North Vancouver City Library

Jonas Clark comes into the bank. "Hetty, my dear," he says. Hetty smiles. "I love you," says Jonas. "Marry me." "Oh, Jonas," says Hetty, "I ... "

Mr Gray comes out of his office. "Who's this?" he says. "Oh, it's Jonas! Oh no, Jonas. My daughter is not for you. She can't marry a poor man. Go away and get some money. Then let's see ... "

Jonas is sad. He walks down the street and into a bar.
He buys a drink and sits down. He wants to get some
money, but how?

Old Harry is sitting near Jonas. There is a bag of gold
on the table. Old Harry is not happy. Two men are
standing above him. They are talking to him. They are
angry. They do not see Jonas.

"Where does this gold come from?" the big man says.
Harry does not answer. "Hit him, Bernie," says the
little man. Bernie hits Harry.
"It's – from Dead Man's River," Harry says. "I can take
you there." Bernie looks at Pete. "I don't like this," he
says. "There are ghosts in Dead Man's River." "Don't
be a fool," says Pete.

Pete and Bernie take old Harry out of the bar. "Take us to Dead Man's River," Bernie says, "or ... " "Yes, yes," Harry says quickly. "Come with me." "Wait," says Pete, "first we're going to the store. We can't take gold from the river with our hands."

Pete and Bernie buy spades and trays for the gold, and also some food. They do not see Jonas behind them.

The three men get on their horses. They ride out of
town along the river. Jonas runs behind them, but they
still do not see him.

The river goes up into the mountains. The men go on
for hours. Then old Harry stops. "It's here," he says.
The men take their spades and trays. They take sand
from the river and wash it. They are looking for gold.

Jonas watches them. Then he goes on, up the river. He takes his spade and his tray. He takes sand from the river and washes it. The sand is brown and grey. He cannot see yellow gold in the sand.

It is late now. The sun is going down. Jonas wants to eat and sleep. But he does not stop. Then he sees two boots in the water beside him. Who is it?

Jonas looks up. Bernie is standing beside him. "Who
are you?" Bernie says. "What are you doing?" He
comes near to Jonas. He puts his hand inside his jacket.
"Has he got a gun?" Jonas thinks.

Jonas stands up. Bernie is very big, and very angry.
Jonas turns and runs. "Don't come back," says Bernie,
"or you are a dead man!"

The sun is going down. Jonas cannot find the road. He listens to the river and stays near it.

What is that? Jonas hears something. He listens. A man is near. A man is calling. A man wants help!

"Where are you?" Jonas calls. "Here! Come here! Help me!" the man answers. Jonas looks behind a big stone. "Harry!" he says.

"What are you doing here?" Jonas asks. "I'm running from Bernie and Pete," Harry says. "But my leg is bad. I can't go on. Bernie and Pete are looking for me. They're angry. There isn't any gold in this river." "What?" Jonas says. "But you ... in the bar ... " "It's not in the water," Harry says. "It's here. Look." He brings out the bags of gold.

"This gold comes from the big river," Harry says. "It's
a hundred kilometres from here. I live near the big
river. I take gold from it. This gold is mine."
Harry's leg is bad. He shuts his eyes. "Help me, Jonas,"
he says. "I can't walk." "Yes, I'll help you," Jonas says.
He puts his arm round Harry. "Come on, stand up," he
says. "I'll take you home."

Jonas hears something. He looks up. A man is coming!
No, not one man, two men! Bernie and Pete! "Wait
here," Jonas says to Harry.
Bernie and Pete are looking under trees and behind
rocks. They want Harry. Jonas watches them. They are
coming near! They have guns! Jonas thinks fast. Then
he takes off his shirt. He puts it on his head.

It is night time, but the moon is bright. Jonas stands up.
"Oo-oo!" he says. Bernie and Pete look at him. They
see a white face and a white head. "I am the dead man
of the river!" Jonas says. "This river is mi-i-ine!"
Now Pete's face is white, too. "Bernie," he says, "Come
on, quick! Run!" He runs. "Oo-oo!" Jonas says again.
Bernie runs, too.

Jonas goes back to Harry. They laugh, and laugh, and laugh. "Now," says Jonas, "I can take you home. Where's your horse?" "It's near the river," says Harry. Jonas gets the horse and Harry gets on it.

"Wait," says Harry. "Give me the gold." Harry takes the bags. Then he gives two to Jonas. "Jonas," he says, "you're a good friend. These are for you."

The next day Jonas goes to the bank. "Hetty," he says,
"do you love me? Yes or no?" "Oh, Jonas," says Hetty,
"I ... er ... yes!" "Then marry me," Jonas says, "But
Father ... " says Hetty. "Hetty," says Jonas, "you can
have your father, or you can have me. Who do you
want?" "You, Jonas," Hetty says. "I want you!"
Jonas takes Hetty in his arms.

The old banker comes in. "Mr Gray," Jonas says, "your
daughter is mine." "But ... " says Mr Gray. "And this
gold is mine, too," Jonas says. "What?" says the banker.
"Where does it come from?" "That's a long story,"
Jonas says. "But it's mine, and I'm a rich man now."
"Jonas, my dear!" Hetty says. "Jonas, my ... er ... son,"
Mr Gray says. They all laugh.

Questions

1 Who is Hetty's father? (*page 1*)

2 Why does Bernie hit Harry? (*page 3*)

3 Why do Pete and Bernie buy spades and trays? (*page 4*)

4 Is it morning or evening? (*page 6*)

5 Who wants Jonas to help him? (*page 8*)

6 Where does Harry's gold come from? (*page 10*)

7 Why does Jonas put his shirt on his head? (*page 12*)

8 Does Hetty love Jonas, or does she love his money? (*page 14*)

Puzzle

1 .... hits Harry.

2 .... has a bad leg.

3 Bernie and .... run from Dead Man's River.

4 Harry gives .... some gold

5 Jonas loves .... Gray.

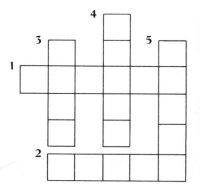

Ideas

1 Take one of the people from the story. Write some sentences about him or her. Do not write his or her name. Now read the sentences to your friends. Ask them who you are writing about.

2 Do you know any ghost stories? Draw a picture to go with a story you know.